STEM
Careers

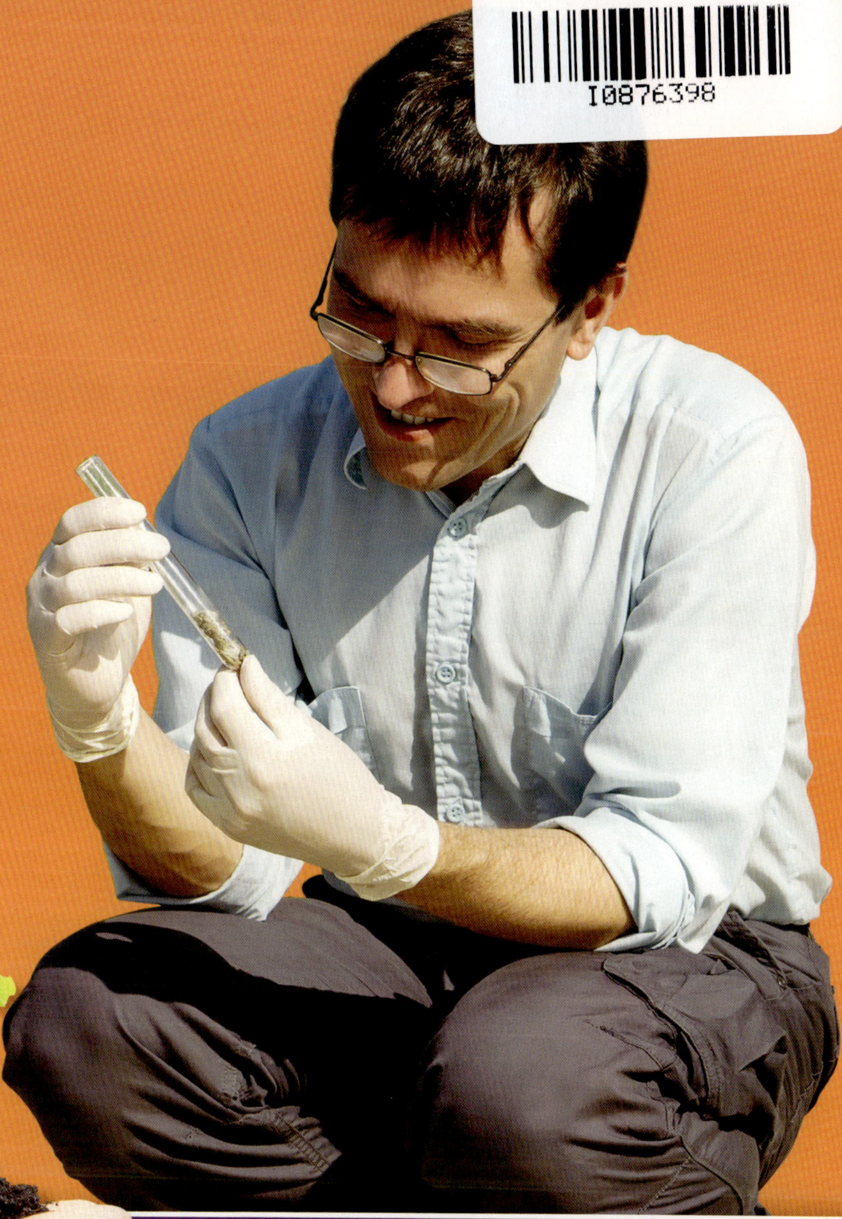

ECOLOGIST

Blaine Wiseman

AV2

www.av2books.com

AV2

Step 1
Go to **www.av2books.com**

Step 2
Enter this unique code
MCEBUN0RQ

Step 3
Explore your interactive eBook!

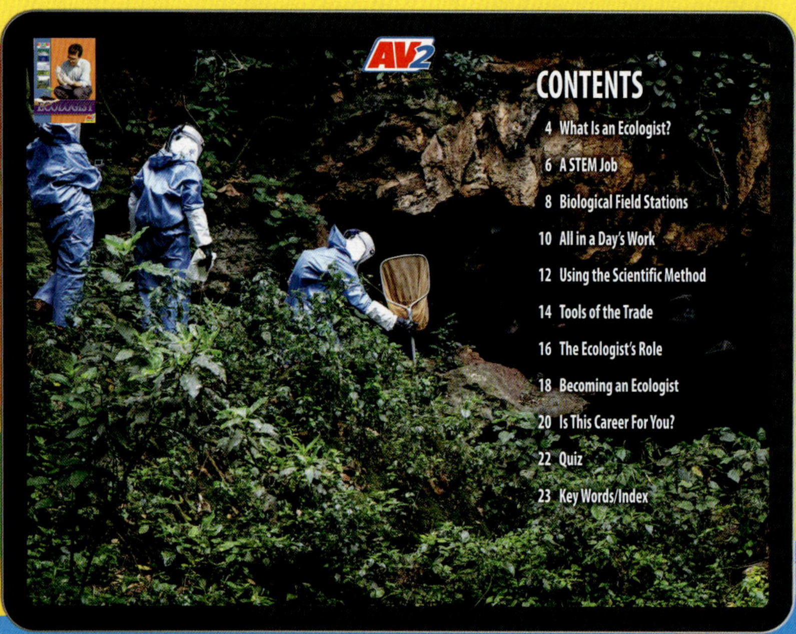

AV2 is optimized for use on any device

Your interactive eBook comes with...

Contents
Browse a live contents page to easily navigate through resources

Audio
Listen to sections of the book read aloud

Videos
Watch informative video clips

Weblinks
Gain additional information for research

Try This!
Complete activities and hands-on experiments

Key Words
Study vocabulary, and complete a matching word activity

Quizzes
Test your knowledge

Slideshows
View images and captions

... and much, much more!

STEM Careers

ECOLOGIST

Contents

What Is an Ecologist?

Ecology is the branch of science that deals with the relationships between living things and their environment. It is sometimes called environmental **biology**. Scientists who study ecology are called ecologists.

Ecologists have knowledge in a variety of scientific areas. They study animals, plants, climate, diseases, air, water, rocks, dirt, and even human activity. An ecologist may examine why an animal lives in a certain environment. He or she may study how a plant's population changes over time. Ecologists can also research the effects a farm has on wild plants and animals in an area.

Ecologists look for patterns and trends that show how and why changes are happening. These patterns and trends show how the world **evolves** over time. Discoveries by ecologists can help humans modify their ways to keep the environment healthy.

The term "ecology" was first used in **1866**, by German zoologist Ernst Haeckel.

The Ecological Society of America (ESA), an organization of ecologists, was founded in **1915**.

The ESA represents more than **9,000** members worldwide.

Ecologists can determine if an environment is healthy by studying the animals and plants that live in it.

A STEM Job

Ecologists work in the **field** of STEM. STEM stands for Science, Technology, Engineering, and Mathematics, or math. STEM is a developing field. Jobs in STEM change as new tools and techniques are created.

Ecology is a science, but ecologists use elements of the other STEM areas as well. They work closely with other members of the STEM community to develop new tools and techniques. Working together helps scientists, technologists, engineers, and mathematicians all get better at their jobs.

Where Ecologists Work

Ecologists often work for universities or governments. Some may also find jobs with environmental groups or private companies. Most ecologists work in states that have a high number of natural areas, such as parks and preserves.

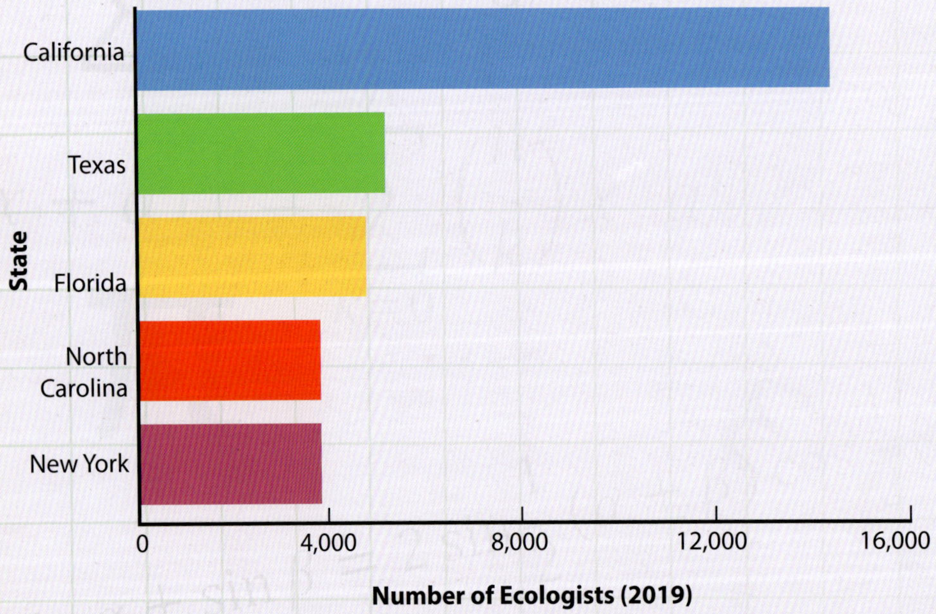

Ecologists rely on other STEM fields in a variety of ways. The tools used by ecologists, such as cameras and microscopes, are made by technologists and engineers. Computer systems, **satellite** tracking programs, and laboratory, or lab, tests rely on science, technology, engineering, and math for accuracy. The changing needs of ecologists can inspire new uses for old technologies, and even new inventions.

Ecologists often use tablets to record data when out in the field.

STEM

People in STEM fields make about **26 percent** more, on average, than those in non-STEM fields.

The average hourly wage for STEM workers is **$38.85**.

15 of the top **20 fastest-growing** occupations in the U.S. require math or science coursework.

By 2025, more than **2 million** STEM jobs in the United States will be unfilled due to a lack of qualified workers.

Biological Field Stations

Ecologists work in a variety of environments and settings. Field work is one of the most important aspects of the work ecologists do. It provides ecologists with the opportunity to research and study plants and animals in their natural **habitats**.

Biological field stations are natural areas dedicated to ecological research. These areas are protected by the government. This allows them to be kept in their natural state.

Biological Field Stations in the United States

There are more than 350 biological field stations across the United States. Most are on land, but some can be found in **marine** environments.

Blodgett Forest Research Station
El Dorado County, California

Alaska Whale Foundation Field Station
Warm Springs Bay, Alaska

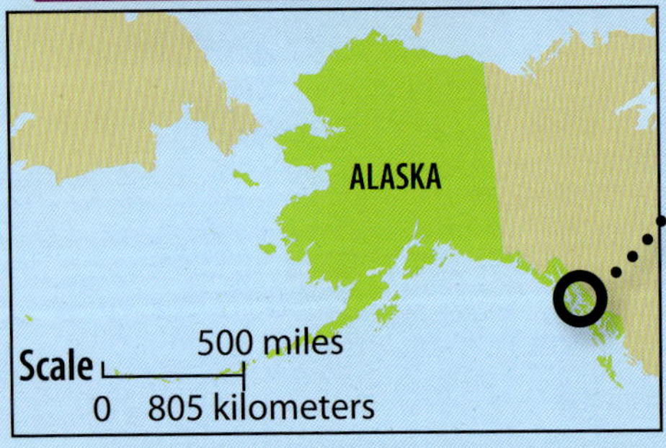

Each biological field station is different. Some are as small as city parks, while others cover thousands of acres (hectares) of wilderness. Field stations usually have classrooms and labs, where students and ecologists can share information and learn about the area and its natural inhabitants. Sometimes, field stations have walking trails with educational signage along the path. Members of the public can walk through the station to learn more about the plants and animals found there.

Ecologists are sometimes invited to conferences to discuss their work with other scientists and the general public.

All in a Day's Work

Some ecologists spend most of their time in the field. Others may spend the majority of their time working in the office, lab, or classroom. Most ecologists divide their time between these settings.

Wherever he or she works, an ecologist's day usually involves gathering data, samples, information, and research. In the lab, ecologists conduct experiments and analyze samples collected in the field. Their office work consists of writing reports and reading scientific journals. Those who teach at colleges and universities will also spend time in their office preparing lectures and lab studies.

Sample Daily Schedule

Ecologists are busy at all times of the year. Their daily tasks depend on many factors. These include the time of year, the weather, and the habits of the animals or plants included in their study. Ecologists must plan their days carefully to ensure their research is done properly.

3:00 AM

An ecologist arrives at a nearby forest to observe bats in their natural habitat. She puts her headlamp on and takes her notepad and camera into the woods. She watches these **nocturnal** animals closely, and records their behaviors on her notepad.

5:00 AM

The ecologist returns to her vehicle to eat breakfast and review the pictures she took. She makes notes on what the pictures show.

8:00 AM

The Sun is now up, allowing the ecologist to see the bat habitat in daylight. She decides to conduct a field **survey**. She makes notes of any changes to the habitat since her last visit.

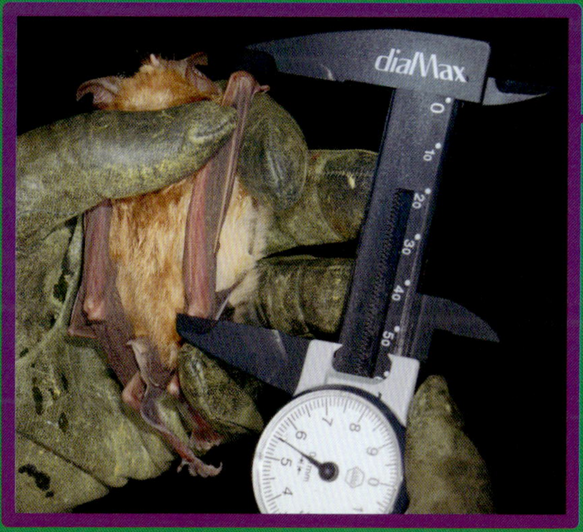

2:00 PM

After a short break, the ecologist drives to her office. There, she uses her notes to start preparing a report about bat behavior.

4:00 PM

The ecologist makes some phone calls to colleagues and other ecologists. She begins planning her evening survey of bats in a different habitat area.

6:00 PM

After dinner, the ecologist sets off to her second field location. As the Sun sets, the bats begin to wake up. The ecologist takes notes on their flying and feeding behaviors. Tomorrow, she will compare this data to the information she obtained in the previous habitat and complete her report.

Using the Scientific Method

Scientists use the scientific method to solve problems. The scientific method is a series of steps. It begins with a question scientists want to answer. First, the scientists find out if someone else has asked the same question. If so, they review that scientist's results and gather information for their work. Next, they make a hypothesis. This is what they think the answer to their question will be. The scientists then test the hypothesis with an experiment. After the experiment, they form a conclusion. This means they study the results and decide if the question was answered. Finally, the scientists share their results with the public and other scientists.

1. Ask a Question

What makes a healthy **ecosystem**?

2. Construct a Hypothesis

Animals use plants for food and shelter. They also need clean air to breathe. Plants provide clean air through **photosynthesis**. Therefore, a healthy ecosystem depends on a balance of plants and animals.

3. Test with an Experiment

Build an ecosystem in a small aquarium or a large jar. Cover the bottom with soil and rocks. Add plants and insects. Make sure the ecosystem is sealed, but that air can flow through.

4. Did the Test Work?

Over a few weeks, the plants should take hold in the soil. The insects should eat the plants. Watch for any changes, such as plant growth, population growth or decline, and **condensation**.

5. Draw Conclusions

After a few more weeks, a healthy ecosystem developed out of a proper balance of plants and animals. The plants grew higher. Condensation formed on the inside of the jar, proving that they were breathing. Holes in the plant leaves indicated that insects were feeding on them.

Tools of the Trade

Specialized tools can help ecologists see their study subjects close up or from a distance. Other tools can help them see their subjects in new ways. These tools help ecologists make important observations.

Motion-Sensing Camera

Wild animals can be difficult to find in their natural habitat. Ecologists place motion-sensing cameras in areas they think animals may live. When an animal comes near the camera, a sensor activates the camera. The camera then takes a picture or video of the animal. This helps ecologists understand animal behaviors and habits.

Satellite Tracker

Satellite trackers use **global positioning system (GPS)** technology. Placing a satellite tracker on an animal lets ecologists know exactly where the animal is at any moment. It also lets them track the animal's movements, allowing them to better understand the animal's behavior.

Time-lapse Technology

Time-lapse technology allows ecologists to study events taking place in an environment in a condensed manner. Processes that take hours, days, weeks, months, or even years to complete, are photographed slowly over a period of time. The photos are then made into a video, which is played back at a faster speed. Ecologists can study how a caterpillar turns into a butterfly or how a glacier recedes in a matter of seconds, even though both processes take much longer to occur.

Computer Modeling Software

Computer modeling software allows ecologists to create **simulations** of events. Some may be programmed to show how air pollution interacts with plants. Others may be designed to assess the risk of a flood in a particular area. The programs allow ecologists to perform experiments that would otherwise take large amounts of time and resources.

Picture This

Photographs are an effective way for ecologists to study plants and animals. Humans have been observing these subjects for thousands of years, but cameras are a much more recent invention.

Then

In the past, ecological researchers found drawing to be one of the best ways to show the features of the plants and animals they were studying. They continued to use drawings as their main method for recording features well into the 20th century.

Now

Modern cameras can capture detailed images instantly. A zoom lens can be used to take closeup pictures from a long distance away. A macro lens can take detailed pictures of tiny objects, such as the body parts of an insect or the patterns on a flower petal. This helps researchers study things they may not be able to see with their eyes alone.

The Ecologist's Role

Ecological studies have led to many important scientific breakthroughs. Public knowledge of ecosystems, evolution, and the **biosphere** all came from ecological studies. A major focus of modern ecological research surrounds issues of **conservation**.

Human ecology is a theory developed in the 1920s. It recognizes the major impact that humans have on the environment. The theory gained popularity during the events that created the **Dust Bowl** of the 1930s. The dust storms that occurred were a result of replacing native grasslands with crops such as wheat and corn. The grasslands had held the topsoil in place. The crops did not. When a drought struck the United States, crops failed, and the soil turned to dust.

The Dust Bowl period forced people to look at how they interact with the environment. Ecologists played an important role in educating the public and developing programs to address environmental concerns. In 1951, a group of ecologists from the ESA formed The Nature Conservancy. This group works to protect natural areas such as grasslands, forests, and rivers from human development. Ecologists have also helped spread knowledge about climate change and its effects on the environment. With this growing knowledge, more than 190 countries have agreed to change their policies, hoping to reverse the effects of climate change.

Ecologists often participate in a type of event called a bioblitz. The aim of a bioblitz is to determine the health of an ecosystem. This is done by locating as many types of plants and animals in an area as possible.

The Nature Conservancy

The Nature Conservancy has grown to become one of the world's largest environmental groups. It currently has a presence in more than 70 countries around the globe.

The Nature Conservancy has more than **1 million** members.

More than **400 scientists**, including ecologists, are employed by The Nature Conservancy.

The Nature Conservancy has protected more than **119 million acres** (48 million ha) of land around the world.

Becoming an Ecologist

Ecologists observe things they see in nature and ask questions to help themselves understand what they see. As children, these people likely showed great interest in watching earthworms come out after a rain shower. They may have wondered how and why sunflowers turn to face the Sun or why raccoons are most active at night. Future ecologists demonstrate a keen interest in animals, plants, and the environment in general.

In school, potential ecologists enjoy science classes. Biology classes give them the opportunity to learn about how living things are created and how they grow and survive. Chemistry classes help them understand how different chemicals affect the environment and everything that lives within it. In geography class, they learn about the world's many natural areas and the issues they are facing. A broad-ranging education is an important starting point for any ecologist.

Ecologist Salaries

Ecologists earn a wide range of salaries. Their income depends mainly on their experience and the type of organization that employs them. An experienced ecologist working for a government agency can make more than $120,000 per year.

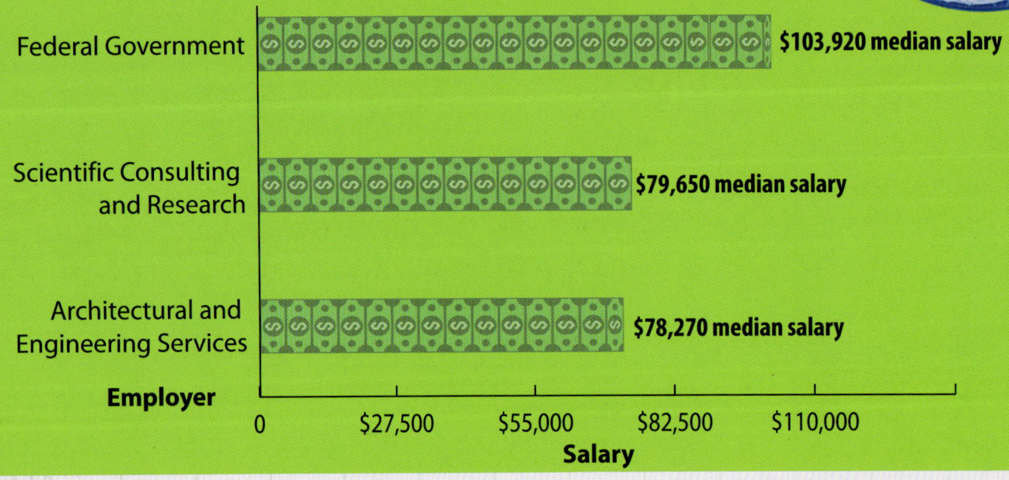

Ecologists are comfortable in outdoor environments. Some venture to remote locations to study the unique ecosystems found there.

Is This Career For You?

People who want to become ecologists should have a passion for learning about the natural world. They should like spending time outdoors, and enjoy studying and researching. Ecologists spend several years in college, and plenty of time learning practical knowledge in the field.

✓ Training

People do not have to wait until college to prepare for a career in ecology. Volunteering is a great way to gain experience in the field. Options to consider include your local zoo, aquarium, or botanical gardens. Helping organizations that work with animals or groups that clean up natural areas can also be of benefit.

✓ Education

Most people interested in becoming ecologists earn a **bachelor's degree** in biology, environmental science, or another field related to ecology. Many then move on to earn **master's degrees** in a more specialized field, such as environmental toxicology. Ecologists in leadership and teaching positions often earn **doctorate degrees**.

✓ Application

Organizations that hire ecologists, such as zoos and national parks, list job openings on their websites. Check online job postings to find out what positions are available. Apply for a postion that matches your skills. Follow up with a request for an interview.

Career Connections

Plan your ecology career with this activity. Follow the instructions in the steps below to complete the process of becoming an ecologist.

A Visit a zoo or nature museum, and request a meeting with an ecologist. Ask questions about the work. Find out where the person studied and how he or she found a job in the field.

B Compare your interests and skills to those of the ecologist. Decide if you still want to pursue a career in ecology.

C Practice and develop the skills ecologists need. Ecologists are patient observers. They know how to look for patterns in nature and take the time to figure out what causes these patterns.

D Go online to find out which colleges have the best ecology programs. Ask them which high school classes you should take to meet their entrance requirements.

1. Look for ways you can gain valuable work experience while you are studying. Seek out volunteer opportunities, **internships**, and entry level positions in the field.

2. Go to ecology-related career fairs. Talk to people who work in ecology. Find out how they started, and ask where their companies post job openings.

3. Follow ecology job sites and related companies on social media. Check online job boards regularly for available jobs. Apply for those that match your experience and skills.

4. When you get a chance to interview for a job, learn everything you can about the organization interviewing you. Make a list of questions about the job. Let the interviewer know why you want the job and what you can offer the organization.

Quiz

1. What is another name for ecology?
2. In what year was the term "ecology" first used?
3. What are the four areas of STEM?
4. Which state employs the most ecologists?
5. What is the name for a natural area dedicated to ecological study?

6. What type of lens allows ecologists to take detailed pictures of tiny objects?
7. What does GPS stand for?
8. What technology helps ecologists watch slow processes quickly?
9. How did ecologists record their subjects before there were cameras?
10. How many members does The Nature Conservancy have?

Answers

1. Environmental biology
2. 1866
3. Science, Technology, Engineering, and Mathematics
4. California
5. Biological field station
6. Macro
7. Global Positioning System
8. Time-lapse
9. Drawings
10. More than 1 million

Key Words

bachelor's degree: the first level of a college program of study

biology: the study of plants and animals

biosphere: the parts of Earth where life exists

condensation: the process that turns water vapor into liquid

conservation: the protection of nature

doctorate degrees: the highest level of college programs of study

Dust Bowl: an area of land where vegetation has been lost and soil reduced to dust

ecosystem: the animals, plants, and non-living things that make up an area or environment

evolves: experiences gradual change

field: a subject area; also the natural environment, rather than a laboratory or office

global positioning system (GPS): a system of satellites that track where objects are located on Earth

habitats: the natural homes of plants, animals, or other organisms

internships: positions in which students learn how a specific job works

marine: found in the sea

master's degrees: the second-highest level of college programs of study

nocturnal: most active at night

photosynthesis: the process plants use to turn carbon dioxide into oxygen

satellite: a machine that moves through space and sends information back to Earth

simulations: models of real activities, created for training purposes or to solve problems

survey: observing, analyzing, and documenting the characteristics of a study area

Index

Get the best of both worlds.

AV2 bridges the gap between print and digital.

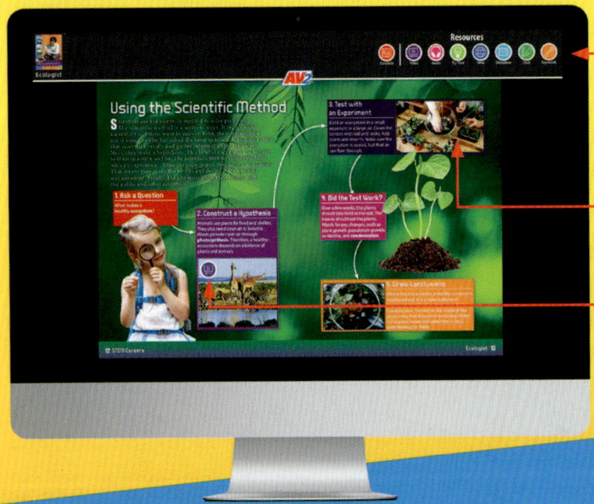

The expandable resources toolbar enables quick access to content including **videos**, **audio**, **activities**, **weblinks**, **slideshows**, **quizzes**, and **key words**.

Animated videos make static images come alive.

Resource icons on each page help readers to further **explore key concepts**.

Published by AV2
14 Penn Plaza 9th Floor
New York, NY 10122
Website: www.av2books.com

Library of Congress Cataloging-in-Publication Data
Names: Wiseman, Blaine, author.
Title: Ecologist / Blaine Wiseman.
Description: New York, NY : AV2, [2021] | Series: STEM careers | Includes index. | Audience: Ages 9-12 |
Audience: Grades 4-6 |
Identifiers: LCCN 2019041053 (print) | LCCN 2019041054 (ebook) | ISBN 9781791116767 (library binding) | ISBN 9781791116774 (paperback) | ISBN 9781791116781 | ISBN 9781791116798
Subjects: LCSH: Ecologists--Vocational guidance--Ju venile literature.
Classification: LCC QH49 .W57 2021 (print) | LCC QH49 (ebook) | DDC 508.023--dc23
LC record available at https://lccn.loc.gov/2019041053
LC ebook record available at https://lccn.loc.gov/2019041054

Printed in Guangzhou, China
1 2 3 4 5 6 7 8 9 0 24 23 22 21 20

052020
101119

Project Coordinator: Heather Kissock
Designer: Ana María Vidal

The publisher acknowledges Getty Images, Alamy, iStock, Wikimedia Commons, and Shutterstock as its primary image suppliers for this title.